ULTIMATE POCKET FUN

Silly Jokes

ARCTURUS

ARCTURUS

This edition published in 2019 by Arcturus Publishing Limited
26/27 Bickels Yard, 151–153 Bermondsey Street,
London SE1 3HA

ISBN: 978-1-78888-479-2
CH006443NT
Supplier: 40, Date 0119, Print run 7769

Printed in the UK

What did the ogre say
when he saw his friend's
monster truck?

I'm green with envy!

HA!

What did the ninja
say to the doctor?

Hi-ya!

What do you call an alligator
that works for the police?

An investi-gator!

Which fruit do twins like best?

Pears!

Why did the Archaeopteryx always catch the worm?

Because it was an early bird!

Knock knock.

Who's there?

Saturn.

Saturn who?

Saturn front of this spaceship, waiting for it to take off!

What do skeletons say before each meal?

Bone appetit!

Teacher: Why are you on the floor in front of Buzz Aldrin?

Student: I asked him if he was the first person on the Moon, and he said, "No, Neil before me."

HA HA HA

What do garbage collectors like to eat?

Junk food!

Did you hear about the elephant that doesn't matter?

It's an irrelephant.

When should you go to see a bird doctor?

When you're puffin!

Teacher: Jake, your essay on "My dog" is exactly the same as your sister's.

Jake: I know, Miss. It's the same dog.

What is the biggest pencil in the world?

Pennsylvania!

How do you make a strawberry shake?

Put it in the freezer!

What do you call a spaceship that doesn't mind its own business?

A prying saucer!

What did the ghost write in his girlfriend's valentine card?

You're simply boo-tiful!

Doctor, I keep thinking I'm Mozart!

I'll be with you in a minuet.

Why do divers approach octopuses very carefully?

Because they're heavily armed!

Doctor, my brother thinks he's an escalator.

Tell him to come and see me.

I can't, he doesn't go up to this floor.

Teacher: Simon, can you say you name backward?

Simon: No, miss!

What do you get if you cross a wizard with a spaceship?

A flying sorcerer!

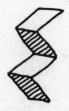

How did the French fries get engaged?

With an onion ring!

How does the king of the jungle spend his days off?

Just lion around!

Do monsters eat snacks with their fingers?

No, they eat the fingers separately.

Why do baby snakes stay close to their parents?

Because a boa's best friend is his smother!

Where do alien fish come from?

Trouter space!

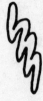

Doctor, I swallowed a bone.

Are you choking?

No, I really did!

Teacher: What's a computer byte?

Samantha: I didn't even know that it had teeth!

What did the spider order at the fast food restaurant?

A burger and flies!

What do you call a monster who is kind to children?

A failure!

Did you hear about the monster that ate a lamp?

It just wanted a light lunch!

What board game do astronauts like best?

Moon-opoly!

HA!

How did the joke about the peanut butter become so popular?

I guess it must have spread!

Did you hear about the hippo at the North Pole?

It got hippothermia!

What did the doctor give to the bird with a sore throat?

Tweetment!

What kind of teacher enjoys morning roll call?

The kind that keeps forgetting names!

A cheeseburger walks into a diner and asks for orange juice.

The waiter says, "I'm sorry, we don't serve food here."

Why did Darth Vader cross the road?

To get to the Dark Side!

HA HA HA

Why is a yeti like an ox that's swallowed a stick of dynamite?

They're both abominable (a bomb in a bull).

Why don't many people pass the test to become a witch?

Because it's very diff-occult!

What did one snake say to the other snake when they split up?

Fangs for the memory!

What's the difference between roast beef and pea soup?

Anyone can roast beef, but have you ever tried to pea soup?

Which birds are found in Portugal?

Portu-geese!

What do you call a gingerbread man with a degree?

A smart cookie!

Did you hear what happened when my friend Ray attacked an alien?

He became an ex-Ray!

Why couldn't the frog put down the book it was reading?

It was just too ribbit-ing!

Doctor, I keep thinking I'm a fish!

You poor sole.

What monster likes cleaning?

The Grim Sweeper!

What's the most important quality needed to become an astronaut?

A good altitude!

What do you get if you cross a shark and an elephant?

Swimming trunks!

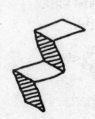

If H_2O is the formula for water, what is the formula for ice?

H_2O cubed!

LOL

How do monster stories begin?

"Once upon a slime ..."

The mechanic asked for a second opinion.

"Okay," said the other doctor. "You're over-tired."

The mechanic told his wife what the doctors had said.

"Hmm," she agreed. "You do seem exhausted."

Knock, knock.

Who's there?

Athena.

Athena who?

Athena alien landing in your yard.

If apples come from an apple tree, and oranges come from an orange tree, where do chickens come from?

A poul-tree.

Little snake: Mama, are we poisonous?

Mama: No, dear, why?

Little snake: I just bit my lip!

Did you hear about the poltergeist in the china shop?

It had a smashing time!

What kind of toilet paper do mathematics teachers prefer?

Multi-ply!

Why did the king visit the dentist?

To get his teeth crowned!

Which monster is really good at science?

Frank Einstein!

What did the doctor say was wrong with the car mechanic?

He'd had a breakdown!

HA!

Why are aliens good for the environment?

Because they're so green!

What do you get if you cross a herd of elephants with a cargo of prunes?

Out of the way!

What do you say if your English teacher is crying?

There, their, they're.

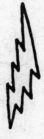

What's the difference between ice cream and milk chocolate?

Anyone can scream, but no one can milk chocolate.

Doctor, I keep thinking I'm an electric eel.

That's shocking!

Did you hear about the vampire that preyed on polar bears?

It got frostbite!

What did one knife say to the other?

Look sharp!

What did the lion say when the zookeeper stopped it from eating a famous poet?

You took the words right out of my mouth!

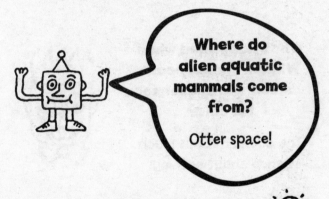

Where do alien aquatic mammals come from?

Otter space!

Teacher: What stays in the corner but travels around the world?

Anna: A postage stamp!

Knock, knock.

Who's there?

Jupiter.

Jupiter who?

Jupiter spaceship on my lawn?

What happened when William Shakespeare visited the doctor for his cold?

The doc said it was much achoo about nothing!

 Where do birds go in the evenings?

To a crowbar!

Why do crocodiles get good grades at school?

Because they can always come up with a snappy answer!

Waiter, will the pizza be long?

No, it will be round!

What directions did the goblin give to the lost ghost?

Go straight, then make a fright at the next turn!

What kind of dog doesn't have a tail?

A hot dog!

Why should you never eat breakfast with an alien?

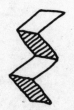

It might contain an Unidentified Frying Object!

Doctor, I always dream there are monsters under the bed.

Saw the legs off the bed, and you'll be fine!

Teacher: What's the chemical formula for water?

Natalie: HIJKLMNO

Teacher: Wrong!

Natalie: Really? Yesterday you said it was "H to O."

What game do you play with a baby ghost?

Peeka-boo!

Why did the hippo go to the doctor?

It was a hippochondriac!

Why shouldn't elephants visit the beach?

In case their trunks fall down!

What did the ghost teacher say to the class?

Look at the board, and I will go through it again.

What's the best way to talk to aliens?

From a long way away!

Why did the boy eat a cupcake each night before bed?

So he could have sweet dreams!

Doctor, I have no energy. I can't even walk down the road without getting tired.

It's because you're wearing loafers!

How do witches race each other?

They ride vroomsticks!

What does a nut say when it sneezes?

Cashew!

Which fruit was said to have launched a thousand ships?

Melon of Troy!

What is William Shakespook's most famous play?

Romeo and Ghouliet!

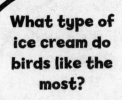

What type of ice cream do birds like the most?

Chocolate chirp!

Why are aliens green?

Because they're not ripe yet!

What do you call a lion that runs a photocopier?

A copycat!

What's a dog's top sweet treat?

Pup-tarts!

Teacher: Sammy, you missed school yesterday, didn't you?

Sammy: Not really!

What do you get if you cross a towel with a spaceship?

A drying saucer!

Where's the safest place to hide from a zombie?

In the living room!

Why are bears so clumsy when they dance?

Because they have two left feet!

Did you hear about the moody dentist?

He was always looking down in the mouth!

What do you call a pattern of stars in the sky that is anxious?

A consternation!

How did the Vikings communicate?

By Norse code!

How do monsters travel on business trips?

By scare-plane!

How do you become a marsupial?

You have to have the right koalafications!

Where do baby cows go for lunch?

The calf-eteria!

Did you hear about the thief who went to the doctor because she couldn't sleep?

The doctor gave her a mat and told her to lie low for a while.

Why didn't the large man know he was overweight?

It just kind of snacked up on him!

What do monsters eat at the beach?

Lice cream!

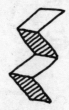

Where does the school furniture go to dance?

To the local desk-o!

What did the star who came last in the shining brightly competition get?

The constellation prize!

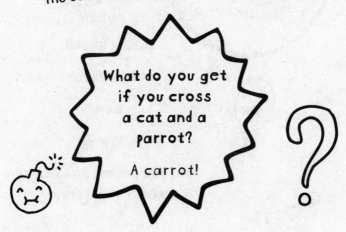

What do you get if you cross a cat and a parrot?

A carrot!

Why did the monster feel sick?

It had eaten some vegetables!

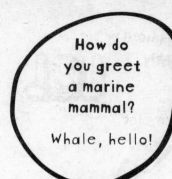

How do you greet a marine mammal?

Whale, hello!

Knock knock!

Who's there?

Ken.

Ken who?

Ken you get me something to eat? I'm starving.

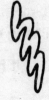

Where do people get their medicine in the countryside?

From a farmer-cist!

Chloë: I wish I had been born a thousand years ago.

Teacher: Why's that?

Chloë: There would be a lot less history to learn!

What party game do ghouls play?

Musical scares!

What do you call a robot who always goes around obstacles?

R2-Detour!

Doctor, I keep stealing things!

Hmm, have you taken anything for it?

Did you hear about the two **IT** teachers who got married?

It was love at first site!

HA!

Why did the tiger cheat on its homework?

Because it was a copycat!

Why did the vampire take up acting?

It was in his blood!

How do you know that an elephant has raided your fridge?

There are footprints in the cheesecake!

Where can you find black holes?

In black socks!

Why did the stand-up comedian go to see the doctor?

He was feeling a little bit funny!

Teacher: Why were you late this morning?

Alex: Because I saw a sign that said, "School Ahead, Go Slow."

How do you stop a werewolf attacking you?

Throw a stick and shout "fetch!"

Where do fish eat their dinners?

At a water table!

What's the best way to see flying saucers?

Trip up a waiter!

Why don't anteaters get ill?

Because they're full of anty-bodies!

What do monsters eat with their cake?

Eyes-cream!

What do alien children do at Halloween?

They go from door to door dressed as humans!

Why couldn't the student write an essay on fish?

He didn't have any waterproof ink!

Why do monkeys love bananas so much?

They're so a-peeling!

Doctor, I feel like a wigwam or a tepee all the time!

That just means you're too tents.

What do they eat at birthday parties in heaven?

Angel food cake!

What do astronauts
wear to weddings?

Spacesuits!

**Which city
was caught
cheating on its
exams?**

Peking!

Why don't witches need dictionaries?

Because they're very good at spelling!

Why did the snake visit the pharmacist?

It needed some asp-irin!

How do you make an apple turnover?

Push it downhill!

What did the aquatic mammal say when it left the party?

I'm otter here!

What happened to the
lion that spent Christmas
by the ocean?

It got sandy claws!

Did you hear the joke about the germs?

I don't want you to spread it around!

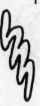

**What did the alien plant say
when it landed on Earth?**

Take me to your weeder!

What do you call a knight who is afraid to fight?

Sir Render!

What do you call a potato standing by the Eiffel Tower?

A French fry!

Why do novelists like to write in cemeteries?

Because there are so many plots there!

What do alien artists paint?

Mars-terpieces!

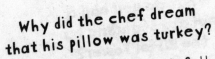

Why did the chef dream
that his pillow was turkey?

Because they're both full
of stuffing!

**Doctor, first my brother was
obsessed with *Tangled*, now he's
totally into *Frozen*.**

How long has he suffered from these
Disney spells?

Dad: Why are your history grades so low?

Lucy: They keep asking about things that happened before I was born!

What did the whale do when it watched a sad movie?

It started to blubber!

What's as sharp and pointed as one of Dracula's fangs?

The other one!

What do you call two matching penguins?

Pengtwins!

What subject do athletes like the best?

Jog-raphy!

HA HA HA

Waiter, there's a wasp in my soup!

I think you'll find it's a vitamin bee, sir.

Doctor, I keep thinking I'm a python.

You can't get around me just like that, you know.

Why couldn't the black hole pass its exams?

Because it's super dense!

What do you call a friendly pharaoh?

A chummy mummy!

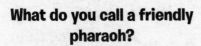

How long does it take a gymnast to get to class?

A split second!

What do you get if King Kong sits on your piano?

Flat notes!

How do you find an alien with one eye?

It's not easy, you should try using both eyes!

Excuse me, what's the quickest way to the hospital?

Lie down on that busy road over there!

What did one frog say to the other?

Time's sure fun when you're having flies!

What do farmers wear to gather their crops?

A har-vest!

Which ice cream do vampires like best?

Vein-illa!

What do you call a spaceship covered in sugar and vinegar?

A sweet-and-sour saucer!

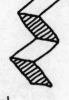

What did the left eye say to the right eye?

Between you and me, something smells!

Why do giraffes have such long necks?

Because their feet smell!

How do bees get to school?

On the school buzz.

What do owls eat for breakfast?

Mice krispies!

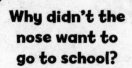

Why didn't the nose want to go to school?

It got picked on!

Doctor, what did the X-ray of my head show?

Absolutely nothing!

Why did the banana go to see the doctor?

Because it wasn't peeling well!

What did the ghost order at the restaurant?

Ghoulash!

Can a monster jump higher than a tree?

Of course it can. Trees can't jump!

What did the insect say before it tried a bungee jump?

Earwig-o!

What did the bucket say to the baby bucket?

You look a little pail!

Waiter, I think I just swallowed a fish bone!

Are you choking?

No, I'm serious!

Why do werewolves get good grades at school?

Because they can always come up with a snappy answer!

What do you call a bowl of melted chocolate flying through space?

A flying saucer!

Teacher: Why haven't you done your science homework?

Luke: Sorry, I'm reading a book about glue, and I just couldn't put it down!

Did you hear about the cannibal lion?

He had to swallow his pride!

Why can't aliens remember anything?

Because everything goes in one ear and out the others!

Did you hear about the rich spiders that got married?

They had an elaborate webbing!

What do you call someone that takes her own salt and pepper everywhere she travels?

A seasoned tourist!

What do you call an alien Santa sleigh?

A UF-Ho Ho Ho!

How do you know if an aquatic mammal is ill?

They have a high beaver!

Why did the music teacher bring a ladder to class?

So her students could reach the high notes!

Knock knock!

Who's there?

Figs.

Figs who?

Figs the doorbell. My hand hurts from all the knocking.

What's small, cuddly, and purple?

A koala holding its breath!

What does an alien use to keep its jeans up?

An asteroid belt!

How do you cut the ocean in half?

You use a sea-saw!

What does the queen do if she burps?

She issues a royal pardon!

What is the stupidest object in the night sky?

The Fool Moon!

How do you take
a pig to the local
hospital?

In a hambulance!

What's sneaky
and flies around
the Earth?

A subtle-ite!

**Where do the
scariest aliens live?**

In a far off, distant
terror-tory!

What did the vegetarian teacher say at lunchtime?

Lettuce eat our salads now!

Why did the baker stop making donuts?

He was bored of the hole business!

Knock knock.

Who's there?

Cows go.

Cows go who?

Cows go "moo" not "who!"

What streaks across the night sky going "kapow, kapow"?

A shooting star!

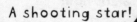

Girl: Do you know who I am? I'm the principal's daughter.

Boy: Do you know who I am?

Girl: No.

Boy: Good.

Doctor, I think I've broken my arm in two places.

Well, don't go back to either of them again.

Knock knock!

Who's there?

Emma.

Emma who?

Emma going to have my dinner now?

What do you call a dinosaur that's been on a diet?

The Lot Less Monster!

Why was the baby ant confused?

Because all his uncles were ants!

What kind of people
eat snails?

Ones who don't like
fast food!

**What TV shows
do germs hate?**

Soap operas!

**What do a cookie and
a computer have in
common?**

They both have chips!

What's yellow and black with red spots?

A leopard with acne!

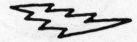

Why were the vampires upside down?

They were just hanging out!

Why is the universe so clean?

Because space is a vacuum!

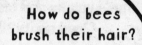

How do bees brush their hair?

They use a honey comb!

Why did the carpenter see a psychiatrist?

He had a screw loose!

What famous city is known as the Big Egg?

New Yolk City!

Have you heard the new joke about the body snatchers?

I'd better not tell it, you might get carried away!

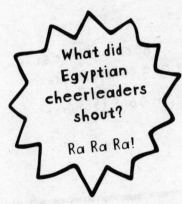

What did Egyptian cheerleaders shout?

Ra Ra Ra!

What do aliens drink their space soda from?

Sunglasses!

Teacher: Anyone who hasn't done their homework will be in big trouble.

Joe: How can we get in trouble for something we didn't do?

Where's the best place to store pizza?

In your stomach!

Where do aliens go to study?

VERY high school!

Doctor, my snoring is so bad, I'm keeping myself awake!

I think you had better sleep in another room!

What do you get if you cross a zombie with a gangster?

Frankenstein's mobster!

What's the difference between a coyote and a flea?

One howls on the prairie, the other prowls on the hairy!

What advice should you always give to robots?

Look before you bleep!

Why did the truck driver stop for a snack?

He saw a fork in the road!

How do smart students travel when they leave school?

On scholar-ships!

What do you call a bug that's see-through?

A glasshopper!

How do you reach the second floor of a haunted house?

Climb up the monstairs!

Why can't a nose be twelve inches long?

Because then it would be a foot!

What time of day do zombies like best?

Ate o'clock!

Doctor, I keep comparing things with something else!

Don't panic, it's just analogy.

What do you call a shooting star that misses the Earth?

A meteor-wrong!

**Where do cats prepare
their meals?**

The kit-chen!

What is the Great Depression?

It's when you get a bad grade in history!

**What's green and slimy and found
in the ocean?**

Whale snot!

Doctor, I keep thinking I'm the king of the jungle.

I think you're lion.

What did the TV presenter say when he saw a herd of buffalo coming over the hill?

Look, there's a herd of buffalo coming over the hill!

Why didn't 4+4 want any dinner?

Because it already 8!

Why did the farmer work his field with a steamroller?

He wanted to grow mashed potatoes!

What did the werewolf say to the skeleton?

It's been nice gnawing you!

Why do some aliens have twisted spaceships?

So they can travel at warp speed!

Why shouldn't you be scared of a six-legged alien?

It's 'armless!

Why did the girl stare at the carton of juice?

Because it said "concentrate."

Why shouldn't you believe what fleas and ticks tell you?

They're all lice.

Which fruit do vampires like to eat?

Neck-tarines!

Why did the art teacher get suspended?

She didn't know where to draw the line!

Doctor, my stomach hurts after eating crabs.

Did they smell bad when you took them out of their shells?

What do you mean "when I took them out of their shells?"

Does Dracula ever eat steak?

Yes, but very rarely!

Doctor, I feel like a cup of tea.

Excellent idea, make me one, too!

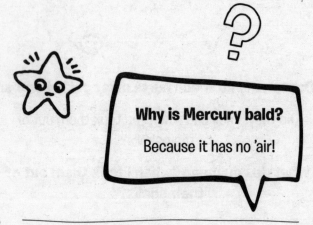

Why is Mercury bald?

Because it has no 'air!

What do you call a kangaroo at the North Pole?

A lost-tralian!

Why was 6 afraid of 7?

Because 7 8 9!

Why did the tofu cross the road?

To prove it wasn't chicken!

Why did the farmer send his cows to the gym every day?

He wanted low-fat milk!

Which monster lives in the forest?

Franken-pine!

What did the doctor pack for her trip to the desert?

A thirst-aid kit!

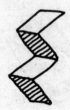

Why was the alien bad at dancing?

It had three left feet!

What do seagulls tell their children before bed?

Ferry tales!

What did the music teacher say to the two students who wouldn't perform together?

Just duet!

What does a monster take for a splitting headache?

Superglue!

What did the alien say when it needed blood tests?

Take me to your bleeder!

What did the ocean say to the river?

Nothing, it just waved!

What keyboard key
do astronauts use
the most?

The space bar!

**What type of socks do
bears wear?**

They don't, they have bear feet!

What do you call someone who loves
hot chocolate?

A cocoa-nut!

English Teacher: Name two pronouns.

Daniel: Who, me?

What's the medical name for a fear of Santa Claus?

Claus-trophobia.

HA!

What do you call a witch at the beach who is too scared to swim?

A chicken sand-witch!

Why did the asteroid stop trying?

He didn't have enough comet-ment!

Why did the cook keep putting the peas through a colander?

He had a re-straining order!

What was the turtle doing on the racetrack?

About ten inches an hour!

Knock knock!

Who's there?

Donut.

Donut who?

Donut ask, it's a secret.

Why was the calendar so popular?

It had a lot of dates!

What do you call an insect on the Moon?

A lunar-tick!

What can run but can't walk?

Your nose!

Where did the leopard have its picnic?

It found just the right spot!

Did you hear about the witch in the five-star hotel?

She ordered broom service!

Did you hear about the gardener who had a cold?

He caught it from the germ-aniums!

What do giraffes have that no other animal has?

Baby giraffes!

What does a headless horseman ride?

A night-mare!

Which vegetables do librarians like?

Quiet peas!

Why did the grape stop in the middles of the road?

He ran out of juice!

Where did the Apollo astronauts go to study?

A Moon-iversity!

Which dessert is never on time?

Choco-late brownies!

What do you get if you cross a parrot and an elephant?

An animal that tells you everything it remembers!

What board game do zombies avoid?

The Game of Life!

What did the sailor say as he threw up on a windy day?

It's all coming back to me now!

What grades do musicians get?

High Cs!

What do you call a bad guy from outer space who is never on time?

Darth Later!

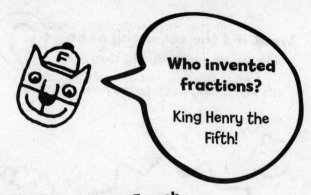

Who invented fractions?

King Henry the Fifth!

Teacher: Do you eat French fries with your fingers?

Student: No, I usually eat them with burgers.

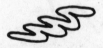

Did you hear about the frog that got taken to the mental hospital?

It was hopping mad!

What's the difference between a rocket and a fly?

A rocket can fly, but a fly can't rocket!

Did you hear about the stranded polar bear?

It was ice-olated!

When does a zombie go to sleep?

When it's dead tired!

**Our teacher talks
to herself.**

So does ours, but she
thinks we're listening!

**Did you hear about
the monster that
listened to classical
music all day?**

It had a suite tooth!

Doctor, I've lost my memory!

When did that happen?

When did what happen?

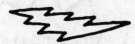

Why was the mushroom invited to a lot of parties?

He was a fun-gi to be with!

Which birds steal soap from the bathroom?

Robber ducks!

Which Egyptian pharaoh
was also an astronaut?

Tutanka-moon!

What did the
daddy ogre say
to his son?

Stop goblin your
food!

Art teacher: What
shade would you
paint a belch?

Rosie: Burple!

HA
HA
HA

What does a toucan wear to go swimming?

A beak-ini!

Doctor, I keep thinking I'm a woodworm.

How boring for you!

Why did the man eat his lunch at the bank?

He loved rich food!

Why were the early days of history called the Dark Ages?

Because there were so many knights!

Which spotted wild cat is angriest?

The cross-alot!

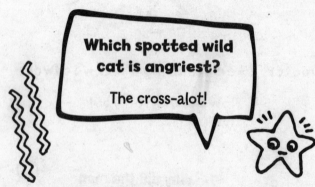

Why did the chewing gum cross the road?

Because it was stuck to the chicken's foot!

What do you call an insect
in a spaceship?

An astron-ant!

Doctor, I think I've been put
together all wrong!

Why do you think that?

Because my feet smell and my
nose runs!

Who saves drowning spirits
at the seaside?

The ghostguard!

Why did the baker work overtime?

She kneaded the dough!

How do you know if you're cross-eyed?

When you can see eye to eye with yourself!

Why do all classrooms have bright lights?

Because the students are so dim!

What do you get if you cross a centipede and a parrot?

A walkie-talkie!

What type of witch can help you see in the dark?

A lights-witch.

What sweet treats do aliens like best?

Martian-mallows!

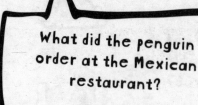

What did the penguin order at the Mexican restaurant?

Brrr-itos!

How many skunks does it take to make a really, really bad smell?

A phew!

Why didn't Socrates like old French fries?

Because they were made in Ancient Greece!

Why was the swamp monster late for work?

He got bogged down in traffic!

The pony's cough is worse.

What do we do?

We take it to a horse-pital!

What do you call a group of freezing planets?

A polar system!

What did the ghost say to the terrified child as it floated across his room?

Don't worry, I'm just passing through!

Doctor, can I get a second opinion?

Of course you can. Come back at the same time tomorrow.

What did the alien race car driver say when it landed on Earth?

Take me to your speeder!

Which legendary concert did cows go to in the 1960s?

Livestock!

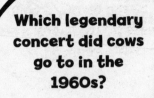

Which snakes are good at equations?

Adders!

How do you get a mouse to smile?

Say cheese!

Why was the mink sent home from school?

It had a bad case of weasels!

HA HA HA

What did the baby dolphin shout when it got caught in seaweed?

Kelp!

What kind of fruit has a bad temper?

A crab apple!

What tool does an arithmetic teacher use the most?

Multi-pliers!

What do you call a haunted hen?

A poultry-geist!

Where do astronauts keep their sandwiches?

In their launch-boxes!

Why did the science teacher get a fake tan?

Because she was a pale-ontologist!

What's the worst game to play with a huge, angry troll?

Squash!

When is the best time to pick apples?

When the farmer is away from home!

Why do astronauts wear bulletproof vests?

To protect themselves against shooting stars!

Why did the birds cry when they heard the story about the peacock?

Because it's such a beautiful tale!

Doctor, there's a man who urgently needs you to tend to scratches all over his body.

What's his name?

Claude!

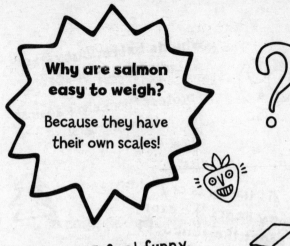

Why are salmon easy to weigh?

Because they have their own scales!

Doctor, I feel funny.

That's hardly surprising— you look hilarious!

What do you get if you cross a robot with a comet?

An aster-droid!

**What did the vampire say
to the invisible man?**

Long time, no see!

**Teacher: What's the definition of
asymmetry?**

Student: A place where you bury dead people.

Waiter, do you serve lobsters here?

Yes, sir, we serve anybody.

Which hotel do mice stay in?

The Stilton!

Sorry I'm late, teacher, I overslept.

What, you mean you sleep at home as well?

Which of Jack Sparrow's feathered friends live in the jungle?

The Parrots of the Caribbean!

How did the astronaut manage to visit the Sun?

He went at night when it wasn't so hot!

What's green and jumpy?

A frog with hiccups!

What do you get if you cross a vampire and a criminal?

A fangster!

How do you make a witch scratch herself?

Take away the "w" to make her itch.

Doctor, I feel like a sheep.

That's baaaaad!

Why do horses eat every day at the same time?

Because they need a stable diet!

Why did the apostrophe grab all the toys?

It was possessive!

How did the wildebeest get down the river?

It paddled its own gnu!

How can you tell the Earth and the Moon are friends?

Because they've been going around together for years!

Doctor, I keep thinking I'm a mosquito.

Don't be such a sucker!

What do aliens do to congratulate each other?

They give each other a high six!

Waiter, there's a slug in my salad!

Don't worry, sir, we won't charge extra.

HA HA HA

What's worse than finding a worm in your school lunch?

Finding half a worm in your school lunch!

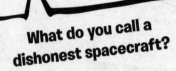

What do you call a dishonest spacecraft?

A lying saucer!

What do you call a kangaroo when it's asleep?

Out of bounds!

How do aliens
count to 50?

On their
fingers!

Why is Britain so wet?

Because the queen has reigned there
for so long!

Why did the astronaut
build her spaceship out of
feathers?

Because she wanted to
travel light-years!

Where do ice cream sellers learn their trade?

At sundae school.

Why did the monster throw up after it ate the priest?

Because it's hard to keep a good man down!

How does a penguin travel across the ice?

It just goes with the floe!

What does a monster give her husband on Valentine's day?

Ughs and kisses!

What do you call a sick extraterrestrial?

An ailin' alien!

Why did the girl study in her bedroom instead of the living room?

She wanted a higher education!

Doctor, I don't think these pills you gave me for heavy sweating are working.

Why not?

They keep falling out from under my arms!

What do you say to bees who try to steal honey?

Oh, beehive yourself!

What's the easiest way to catch a fish?

Ask someone to throw it to you!

When is it easy to beat a zombie in an argument?

When it has no leg to stand on!

Why did the astronaut fly into the black hole?

He didn't understand the gravity of the situation!

Why did the tired athlete run around and around her bed?

To catch up on some sleep!

Teacher: What was the Romans' greatest achievement?

Jordan: Learning to speak Latin!

Why did the boy give mustard to his poodle when it had a fever?

Hot dogs are always better with mustard!

Why don't cheetahs wash?

They don't want to be spotless!

What do spooks put their drinks on?

Ghosters.

HA!

What did the martial artist buy from the butcher?

Karate chops!

Doctor, I think I'm a dog!

How long have you felt like this?

Ever since I was a puppy!

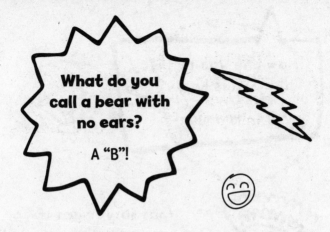

What do you call a bear with no ears?

A "B"!

What did the alien cat say when it landed on Earth?

Take me to your litter!

Why was the clock in the school cafeteria slow?

Because it always went back four seconds.

How can you tell if
the Sun is happy?

It's beaming!

What do you get if you
cross a rooster and a bell?

An alarm cluck!

Why did the miniature tool
go to see the doctor?

It was a little saw.

HA
HA
HA

Which Roman Emperor suffered from hayfever?

Julius Sneezer!

What do you get if you cross a parrot and a lion?

A bird that talks your head off!

What do ancient Egyptian monsters call their parents?

"Mummy and Deady"!

What do alien poets write?

Uni-verses!

Doctor, no matter what I do, I just can't get to sleep!

Lie on the edge of the bed, and you'll soon drop off.

How did the egg get up the mountain?

It scrambled!

How do ghosts make themselves heard in a crowd?

They use a loud-spooker!

What time do ducks get up?

At the quack of dawn!

Teacher: Can you name ten dinosaurs?

Ben: Yes, eight *T. rex* and two *Stegosaurus*.

Why are the tonsils excited?

They've heard the doctor is taking them out on Friday!

Why did the firefly get bad test results?

It wasn't very bright!

Why did the pig kidnap the farmer?

To save his own bacon!

What does an oversized alien wear?

A not-very-much-space suit!

Why shouldn't you talk to rabbits about vegetables?

Because they don't carrot all!

Why did the banshee marry a pirate?

So she could wail the seven seas!

Who do warlocks see when they are feeling sick?

The witch doctor!

Who's in charge of Monster City?

The night-mayor!

Why did Mickey Mouse go to Neptune?

He was looking for Pluto!

What do you call a spaceship made out of herbs?

A thyme machine!

Waiter, there is a spider on my plate. Call the manager at once!

That won't do any good, sir. She's afraid of them, too.

Dad: Did you come first in any of your school subjects?

Daisy: No, but I was first out of the classroom when the bell rang!

HA!

Why couldn't the butterfly go to the dance?

It was a moth ball!

What type of dog does a vampire have?

A bloodhound!

Why did the geometry teacher stay home from class?

She'd sprained her angle!

Did you hear about the man who lost his left side in an accident?

Don't worry, he's alright now!

What do dogs eat at the movies?

Pup-corn!

Which star do you get if you crush an insect?

Betelgeuse!

What nation do geography teachers love best?

Expla-nation!

What did the doctor give to the nervous elephant?

Pills to keep him trunkquil!

Why did the robot never feel sick?

It had a cast iron stomach!

HA HA HA

How many more times do I have to tell you to walk away from the cupcakes?

None, I've eaten them all now!

How can you tell if an alien has used your toothbrush?

It tastes like alien spit!

Why do Frankenstein's monster's arms squeak?

Because he ran out of elbow grease!

On what day was the hairy monster born?

Fursday!

What do nuclear scientists have for dinner?

Fission chips!

What did the dentist say when her plane hit turbulence?

Brace yourself!

Why don't people laugh at gardeners' jokes?

Because they're too corny!

What's the best time to buy a canary?

When it's going cheep!

Why aren't there any desks in the mathematics classroom?

Because they use times tables!

Did you hear about the pig that lost its voice?

It was disgruntled!

What do you call a reindeer with no eyes?

No eye-deer!

What do you call a reindeer with no eyes or legs?

Still no eye-deer!

What's a ghoul's best-loved dessert?

Strawberries and scream!

If astronauts breathe oxygen during the day, what do they breathe at night?

Night-rogen!

Why is the library always a school's tallest building?

Because it has the most stories!

Why did the chicken cross the ocean?

To get to the other tide!

Why did the reindeer run around in circles?

Because it was in Lapland!

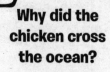

What do snowmen eat for breakfast?

Frosted flakes!

What did the boat's captain do when he was sick?

He went in to see the dock!

Why did the astronomer change his mind about the Sun after looking at it through an ultraviolet telescope?

He saw it in a whole different light!

What's green, has two heads, and goes up and down?

An alien stuck in an elevator!

How do you treat
an alien with
claustrophobia?

Give it some space!

**What kind of music do
astronauts like?**

Rocket 'n' roll!

HA!

What's it like to
have a monster as
a pilot?

Terror-flying!

What's wet, striped, and goes bump-bump?

A zebra in a clothes dryer!

Waiter, my plate is wet!

I think you'll find that's the soup.

Teacher: What is the shortest month?

Sarah: May. It only has three letters!

What did the little ghost say to his best friend?

"Do you believe in people?"

Doctor, I feel like a spoon.

Lie down and don't stir.

What's the best way to get in touch with a fish?

Drop them a line!

How do you impress an art teacher?

Easel-y!

What do you call a genuine spacecraft?

A True-FO!

When should you take a cookie to the doctor?

When it feels crumby!

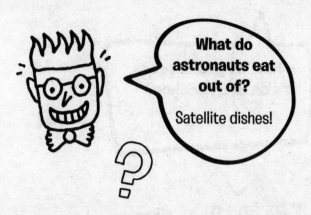

What do astronauts eat out of?

Satellite dishes!

What did the science teacher say before he got into a fight?

Let me atom!

Why did the girl want to kiss Dracula?

She was batty about him!

What's the difference between a buffalo and a cookie?

You can't dunk a buffalo in your milk!

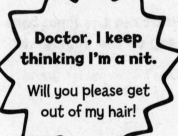

Doctor, I keep thinking I'm a nit.

Will you please get out of my hair!

What did the girl star say to the boy star?

I really glow for you!

What's the medical term for a parrot that has lost its memory?

Polynesia!

What did the limestone say to the geologist?

Don't take me for granite!

Did you hear about the girl who was smacked in the face by a frisbee?

She wondered why it was getting bigger ... and then it hit her!

What are vampires most afraid of?

Tooth decay!

How can you spell the name of a hungry insect using just three letters?

M. T. B.

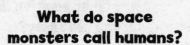

What do space monsters call humans?

Breakfast, lunch, and dinner!

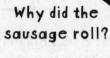

Why did the sausage roll?

Because it saw the milk shake!

Did you hear about the man who was hit on the head by an icicle?

It knocked him cold!

Gym teacher: What position do you play?

Bob: I've been told I'm the main drawback, sir.

Why did the polar bear return some food to the supermarket?

Because the seal was broken!

Why should a mummy be careful on its day off?

So it doesn't unwind too much!

Teacher: What is a light-year?

Pupil: The same as a normal year—but with fewer calories?

How many ears does Captain Kirk have?

Three—a right ear, a left ear, and a final frontier!

Why was the computer virus so serious?

It was terminal!

What starts with "T," ends with "T," and is full of "T"?

A teapot!

HA!

Where did the ruler Montezuma study?

At Az Tech.

Why is it difficult to tell twin witches apart?

Because you don't know which witch is which!

What is large and has three trunks?

An elephant going abroad!

What do you give sick insects?

Anty-biotics!

What did the pencil sharpener say to the pencil?

Stop going around in circles, and get to the point!

What do you call a bad guy from outer space walking in the sea?

Darth Wader!

HA HA HA

What did the porcupine say when her son sat on her knee?

Ouch!

Did you hear about the single monster who tried online dating?

She was looking for an edible bachelor!

Waiter, there's a dead fly in my soup!

Sorry, madam, are you a vegetarian?

What do you say to an alien with two heads?

Hello to you, and hello to you, too!

What do you call a 12-foot monster with claws?

"Sir!"

What's the relationship between past, present, and future?

Tense!

Doctor, I keep getting pains in my eye when I drink hot chocolate.

Have you tried taking the spoon out of your mug?

Did you hear about the snakes' valentine?

They sealed it with a hiss!

Did you hear about the hilarious banana?

It had the whole fruit bowl in peels of laughter!

Planet: Are you joking?

Star: No, I'm Sirius!

Doctor, everything I touch turns to gold!

Don't worry, it's just a gilt complex.

What party game do monsters like best?

Swallow the leader!

Why did the leopard miss so many dances?

He kept breaking out in spots!

Knock knock!

Who's there?

Carla.

Carla who?

Carla restaurant, I'm hungry!

Why did the sickly crab walk sideways?

Its medicine had side effects!

What do you call a space telescope that doesn't work?

Hubble trouble!

Why did the baker get fired from her job?

She was a loafer!

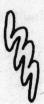

Which dessert makes the swamp monster lick his lips?

Key slime pie!

Matthew: I just banged my head on my desk.

Teacher: Have you seen the school nurse?

Matthew: No, just stars.

Doctor, I feel like a piece of cake!

Yes, you do look a bit crummy

How do bees celebrate moving to a new place?

With a house-swarming party!

Why did the music teacher have to miss school?

He was a trebled man!

Why should you never boil a space telescope?

Because it might Hubble over!

What's the best cure for graphite poisoning?

Pencil-lin!

What do birds grow on?

Egg plants!

Why wouldn't the oyster twins share?

Because they were two shellfish!

What do monsters eat with their sandwiches?

Ghoulslaw!

What does a builder use to fix the ape house at the zoo?

A monkey wrench!

What can you catch but never throw?

A cold!

HA HA HA

Teacher: Do you know why your grades are so bad?

Nathan: I can't think.

Teacher: Exactly!

What do astronauts put
in their sandwiches?

Launch-meat!

Knock knock!

Who's there?

June.

June who?

June know what time dinner is?

What is a vampire's best-loved sport?

Bat-minton!

Why did the headless ghost go to see the doctor?

Because he wasn't all there!

Why didn't the alien eat the clown?

He said it tasted funny!

What happened when the girl vampire met the boy vampire?

It was love at first bite!

Why are camels so good
at hide-and-seek?

Because of their
camel-flage!

Knock knock!

Who's there?

Lettuce.

Lettuce who?

Lettuce in, and you'll find out!

**Why did the student walk to school
facing the wrong way?**

It was "back-to-school day"!

What do astronomers like to chew?

Hubble gum!

What award does the dentist of the year receive?

A little plaque!

How do you make a skeleton laugh?

Tickle its funny bone!

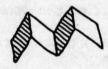

What did the lion cub say to its mother?

Every day I love you roar and roar!

Waiter, is there pizza on the menu?

No, madam, I just wiped it off.

Teacher: What's the best thing about school?

John: Coming home again!

What's the coldest country in the world?

Chile!

Knock knock!

Who's there?

Dishes.

Dishes who?

Dishes me. Who's that?

What did the midwife say when she delivered quads?

Four crying out loud!

Why do skeletons find it easy to stay calm?

Because nothing gets under their skin!

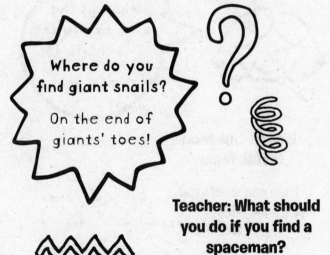

Where do you find giant snails?

On the end of giants' toes!

Teacher: What should you do if you find a spaceman?

Student: Park in it, man!

Why do hummingbirds hum?

Because they don't know the words!

HA!

What did the paper say to the pencil?

Write on!

Waiter, this food tastes funny.

Then why aren't you laughing?

Doctor, I keep thinking that I'm a dog!

 Climb up on the couch, and I'll take a look at you.

But I'm not allowed on the couch!

What do you call the lights on a lunar spacecraft?

 Moonbeams!

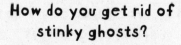

How do you get rid of stinky ghosts?

With scare freshener!

Why should you tell jokes to a ghost?

To lift her spirits!

Teacher: Why does your homework look like your dad wrote it?

Emily: Because I used his pen!

HA HA HA

Doctor, would you say I have a split personality?

One at a time, please!

Why couldn't the farmer water his garden?

There was a leek in his bucket!

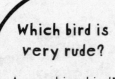

Which bird is very rude?

A mockingbird!

What steps should you take if you see an alien?

Large ones!

What do you call spaghetti in disguise?

An impasta!

Why did the astronaut throw eggs at the alien?

He wanted to eggs-terminate it!

Which monster is horribly untidy?

The Loch Mess Monster!

Teacher: Have you been stupid all your life?

Andrew: Not yet!

Which side of a porcupine is the prickliest?

The outside!

Doctor, I'm suffering from really bad deja vu!

Didn't I see you yesterday?

What did the llama say when it was invited to visit Spain?

Alpaca my suitcase!

Doctor, everyone thinks I'm a liar.

I can't believe that!

Shakespeare walked into a diner and asked for a drink.

The man behind the counter shook his head and said, "You're Bard."

What day of the week do ghosts
look forward to?

Fright-day!

**Teacher: I wish you would pay a
little attention.**

Jack: I'm paying as little as I can!

What kind of horse would you ride
on the Moon?

A-pollo pony!

Knock knock!

Who's there?

Annie.

Annie who?

Annie chance of getting something to eat?

Doctor, I keep running around pretending to be a seabird.

No wonder you're puffin!

What's the fastest country in the world?

Rush-a!